White Summer

CRAB ORCHARD AWARD SERIES IN POETRY

First Book Award

White Summer

Summer

JOELLE BIELE

Crab Orchard Review

& Southern Illinois University Press

CARBONDALE AND EDWARDSVILLE

Printed in the United States of America

05   04   03   02   4   3   2   1

The Crab Orchard Award Series in Poetry is a joint publishing venture
of Southern Illinois University Press and *Crab Orchard Review.* This series
has been made possible by the generous support of the Office of the
President of Southern Illinois University and the Office of the Vice
Chancellor for Academic Affairs and Provost at Southern Illinois
University Carbondale.

Crab Orchard Award Series in Poetry Editor: Jon Tribble

Text design by Erin Kirk New

Library of Congress Cataloging-in-Publication Data

Biele, Joelle, 1969–
White summer / Joelle Biele
p. cm. — (Crab Orchard award series in poetry)
I. Title. II. Series.

PS3619.I535 W48 2002
811'.6—dc21
ISBN 0-8093-2468-7 (paper : alk. paper)   2002018991

Printed on recycled paper. ♻

The paper used in this publication meets the minimum requirements
of American National Standard for Information Sciences—Permanence of
Paper for Printed Library Materials, ANSI Z39.48-1992. ∞

For Kirk

Contents

Three

Acknowledgments

Grateful acknowledgement is made to the editors of the following journals, in which poems from *White Summer* first appeared, some in slightly different form:

Antioch Review—"Autumn" and "The Festival of Dolls"
Epoch—"Hopkins' Clouds"
Hubbub—"Wedding Kimono"
Indiana Review—"The Feast of Saint Joseph"
The Iowa Review—"Rapture"
Meridian—"Grand Central"
Nimrod—"Night Sky"
Phoebe—"Winter"
Poetry Society of America Newsletter—"Patapsco Female Institute"

One

Autumn

I think it was October, November,
morning, dark, along a bend in the Wolf
or Wisconsin River, and I am seven

or eight, and we are sitting on the cold hood
of my father's car, the first days
of the fall migration, and I am sure

it was the long-necked cranes, nothing like
the cranes I folded from paper
at school. I know the changed leaves muddy

the water, and the marsh grass, dry,
lost, takes on a kind of metal brilliance,
hard from the river, and the early sun.

I am tired and want to go back
in the car, the radio night, far from here,
and I am thinking of my mobile,

the birds I tied to a hanger,
triangle out of triangle, wing, neck, spine,
their bodies full of air. I don't hear the wings,

I don't hear the calls, only the rush
of cattails, mildew, ferns, and a sky
full of birds. It was like a giant string

pulled them up, could pull me up, into the air,
a wingspan bigger than my boy's body,
into the pull of earth turning, the rhythm

of light, the pattern of stars, a map,
a grid, a night city or late orchard
I could hide in, apples filled with stars.

The Festival of Dolls

The shiny crown, the toy sword,
the wooden scepter, the emperor
with his little black cap staring down
from the highest shelf, his empress hiding
behind her fan: Keiko's house was like that,
like looking at another country, a mixture
of chrysanthemum, pine, and peach,
and I stood a long time bundled
in my winter coat looking at the dolls.
I loved going there, loved looking,
each one sitting perfectly in place, each one
graceful and sure, each one looking at me,
telling me to sit perfectly still,
pure and light like blossoms strewn
from a tree, maids in waiting, absence
of body. There were musicians with
real drums and flutes that really played,
palace guards and attendants carrying
umbrellas and shoes, everything starched
and damask, all of them thinking
of the oxcart and painted palanquin,
their long journey, the prairie night,
into spring. We gave them wine and fruit
in nested boxes on tiny banquet trays
and sat on the living room floor
for cups of sweet sake and diamond-shaped cakes,
candy we ate with the wrappers on
and fairy bowls of rice and beans,
both of us eating, both of us laughing,
a child's imperial feast, the silent dolls,
drinking from flowers, birds carved from air,
better than jade, a bracelet of coral.

Grand Central

As if the night sky could be this dirty shade
of green and the stars were just these small,
small lights, here's a night sky no one ever sees,
the lion, the fish, the bear—the yellow lines
that blend in the dark like words in the soft pages
of children's books. I'm waiting for my father,
sitting on the steps or the long wooden bench,
its high back, watching the attendant,
his quiet face and blue cap. I don't know
if my father's late or maybe I'm early—
there's the damp newspapers and muddy shoes,
lilies and ferns, a cart of summer flowers.
The station almost empty, the trains
an hour apart, I know there's a string quartet
around which people stand in a sort of circle—
they're tired but listening—and there's a woman
trying to get someone to dance, as if
this is what she's wanted to do her entire life,
as if this is what she's been doing, the station
to herself, until someone finally steps in,
and now I'm afraid to look. There's the man
who once took my book and drew the folded hands
of Jesus on the inside cover, the woman
who gets on trains every night asking
for fare, the man who'll come up,
embrace you, a beery kiss on the ear.
If it's true, they've already entered
the afterlife, if it's what gives them
that lightness, that ability to disappear,
then all I hear is the roll of the board
like so many shutters banging, like birds,
like people clapping their hands. Rain outside,
it's a sparrow night, all the black umbrellas,
and under any one I can meet my father.

If this is how one enters the afterlife,
just a cello and water on the floor,
the gritty sound of arrivals and departures,
a woman with a bucket and brush on the stairs,
then the revolving door is the ocean,
the white tail of the salty wind,
and I'm standing on the hill, watching
the stars, the trains, the long black whistle,
the dirty waters of somebody's empty heart.

Langestrasse

For two weeks he stood on the edge of the square,
his curly black hair hiding his eyes,
stood away from the raffle stands, the book stalls,

the musicians in their corners.
In one hand he holds the reins of a pony
like a toy left in the rain, in the other

an empty silver cup, a tattered bouquet.
He stands stiffly, defiant, an adze's bold strokes
shaping his cheeks and the back of his neck.

He could have come in by the sea,
tossed off one of the shifting islands, walked
across the moors, down the sandy lanes

lined with yellowing birches and salty leaves.
The clouds rush like pieces of linen pulled through a ring.
Mist in the air, it's as if inside the boy were flying,

as if inside he were running through the wind,
his coat stretched out behind him, as if he were
leaving his body or trying to get back in.

Rapture

It starts with a low rumbling, white static,
a broken shell to the ear. It starts with water,

tide pulling. It starts with the cold kiss of the sun.
It's hands clapping, birds clamoring,

and laughter coming through the walls.
It starts with snow breathing,

bottles falling, the night hum of a road.
It's a bus shifting gears.

It's the flower inside the tree, the song
inside the wood. It's a mouthpiece buzzing,

the *psh-psh* of a Bach cantata.
It's walking through a pile of leaves.

It starts with wet legs and poppies.
It starts with bitter chicory.

It's diked fields, the suck under your shoe.
It starts with an idling motor. It's horses in fog.

It starts with spilt sugar. It's sizzle and spatter.
It's your voice under water. It's a bell buoy's sway.

It starts with a sail luffing, whispering
in the wings. It starts with a policeman walking,

a rosy ear, a dog barking, honey and flies.
It starts with a knife sharpening

and plates smashing against the door.
It starts deep in the belly, the back of the throat.

It's a need like salt, crackle and flame.
It starts with sounds you've never made.

It's not your voice in your mouth.
Your words are not your own.

It's the body breaking into islands.
It's the fall through wind lifting white leaves.

Patapsco Female Institute

The first steps you take lead to nowhere.
The front stairs don't even reach the front door.
The building's been stripped of all usable
parts—shutters, windows, frames—not even
a rotting board or broken door to sway
above you. From here, on the steps, you can
see where the second floor must have reached—
the outer wall fallen away—and you can draw
in the rooms. The ceiling opens on rain.
Make it Greek, but American, too. Make it
antebellum, but after the war. This was once
Ellicott City's biggest house on Ellicott City's
biggest hill. So throw in some heavy
velvet curtains for warmth, and sketch
a weather vane on the roof for luck.
Here, girls must have stood watching
boats sail down the river, loading or
unloading, freight trains' smoke high in the trees.
Go down on the lawn where they must have
practiced dancing, lifting boughs of ivy
up and over each other, or taking the lead—
the insignificant detail—to make it
look easy was key. The colors endure
like handprints on brick, each one for the life
spent waiting, for the life spent high on the hill.
The mind searches these places out,
it may dwell here, or in a building like it,
high above a river that floods every fall,
in a town, like this one, that never recovers
its losses. To survive means *to live beyond*.
The imagination translates what's vast
and vacant beyond the other side
of the mind in the half-world that makes this one
seem more real. Nothing loves ruin more

than a house. Nothing wants to be more
than a house than this one where girls were
broken into women, broken into
their bodies, where down the hill the river
flowed steady and sure, fluent like a hand
sliding down the back or like a hand
slamming down hard. The trees have stained
in the rain, and tonight the rain will freeze.
If it's true that the eye is not satisfied
with seeing, nor the ear filled with hearing,
and that we will always forget, then
desire may be our greatest failing, but today
the season is a house of possibility.

The Field

And then when you least expect it,
you're back on the bridge, driving
over the river, cold, tired, that gathers
the silt of a poor delta, driving west
from Baton Rouge to Plaquemine,
sweet smoke on the horizon, fields
of burning cane, and suddenly
you can see your future, neither here
or there, but always moving where nothing
connects. One day you live on a piece
of land as flat and stiff as a board,
and the next you wake in a house
so damp you're convinced the house
is under water. Some drown when they fall
into a night like that. To make a pattern
of this life you might as well unfold
a map, trace the roads stretching across
the page, now and then lift your hand as if
the lines could somehow tell a story
and the mind accept the life through language.
In a warm fall everything is exaggerated,
even the trees, and memory can be obscured
like an azalea too red to remember.
You remember so little—shapes, colors,
names—a place outside time—too brief
to imagine but marking you for good
like the leaves coming down still green,
unchanged, too much wet sun and moss,
and the night air does not drop into the day.
There are times when the lyric is too much,
when it breaks down word by word and sound
by sound. It's what we want the afterlife to be,
that first flash of fire from the train window,
the men gathered around the flames that put you back

13

on the bridge, cane scattered over the road,
the men waving from the truck, heading into
the fields, the two-block towns, the clapboard church,
the plastic windows, back on River Road,
the levee, the pale, sleeping fields.

The Wren

So they'd go down the lanes with sticks and switches,
knobbed pieces of wood swinging from their hands.
They'd go down singing on both sides of the hedges,

hitting dry branches and snapping off twigs.
To chase the wren from its nest, they'd shoot
toy rifles, their fathers' pistols,

not touching the nest or they'd forfeit salvation.
Sometimes they'd spare it, deck its legs and neck
with their sisters' ribbons, and sometimes on a pile of ivy

or tied to a holly with a bottle of spirits,
they'd take it to town or one boy parading,
the bird in a cage. Or not a cage

but a stable lantern, a carved-out turnip,
or matchbox, or a house with windows and doors,
glass squares at both ends carried between two hoops

or in a hoop or on two poles carried by four men
who said it was a heavy weight and called it *Noah's Ark*.
There could be sticks in the shape of the cross,

a tiny Christ, a procession with drums beating,
colors flying, and the feathers traded for coins or kisses,
a few sips of beer, the other boys singing *Knock at the knocker*,

ring at the bell. Then there'd be a pig's bladder inflated,
maybe a cow's, a fool ready to strike anyone lining the street
followed by women dressed as goats,

men wearing women's blouses stepping with canes,
a wooden horse, its snapping jaws, two boys under
like a galloping dragon, a battle of paper swords and straw.

Sometimes the first to catch the wren was called the king,
and with torches and fifes, his band chalked the year,
Vive le Roi, on village doors before heading to Mass,

the bird on a pillow of leaves, mistletoe
if they could find it, to offer the priest,
because it was St. Stephen's Day, December 26,

the only day for hunting the wren.
Some said it was to punish the bird for waking
Stephen's jailer when he went to escape,

and some said it was for waking Christ's guards in the garden.
Some said it was for warning the Danes of the Irish approaching,
or was it King William's army by hopping on a drum?

Then there's St. Moling's curse after a wren ate his fly:
He that marred for me the poor pet that used to be making music,
let his dwelling be forever in empty houses

with a wet drip therein, and let children and young persons
be destroying him. Fishermen said a sea sprite haunted the shoals
so they kept a wren in their boats to ward off a wreck,

and others said the bird brought fire, was Mary's pet,
the wren who skulks in bushes, whose body once told the future,
whose song was outside the church, the wren who cocks his tail feathers

and tilts his wings, the winter wren who is the tiny king,
the king of the brambles, the king of the cold,
the wren who is the king's fowl, the king of the thorns,

the king of the snow. With your brown body
barred and mottled black, the Greeks called you
cave dweller for your deep secret nests,

and Shakespeare *wren, with little quill.*
You are the bird called *little nettle, little oxen eye.*
You've been singing all evening with the clouds wandering

over the yellowing fields, buttercups and clover,
singing over the broken walls with the bells from the church,
singing the hours to the barns and the fences,

singing like the shallow river that curves under the oaks,
singing like stones, like violets and foxglove,
singing the hills into being with the sharp bristling light of your song.

Verviers

He sits across the aisle, shoes off,
a red and white shawl around his neck.
Still a boy, a new prayer book on his lap,

he reads aloud, but softly, so at first,
I don't hear him, only the slight rise
and fall of the fields outlined with black trees.

His voice comes to me like the one I heard
every day at noon, the creek turning
through the valley under my window,

the kingfisher darting over the surface,
resting above one of its rocky pools.
It's as if the boy can hear something else,

as if the men can straighten the tracks like a song
and the nests trace the patterns of the stars.
When I was small my brother and I rode our bikes

into the graying fields and put our ears
to the rails. We heard nothing but the wind
and the birds heading for the cold DuPage.

Although I know the little towns are only
laundry on the line, geese in the yard,
some pails under blighted apple trees,

I want to know what he knows: these fields,
full of water, are brighter than they really are,
their bristly green of nettles and stings,

the long lines of birds brushing the river north.
The car is crowded and warm, and after
Liège, almost full. A woman and child

sit next to him. He stops, reads only
to himself and before anyone
can look again, puts his book away.

Family Stories

Some stories will never leave you alone.
They work their way into the blood, the brain,
they flash in corners of your dreams
with laundry drying in the halls,
lemon oil rubbed into wood, bristles and soap
working their way under your nails until it's your arm
in the winter Hudson, the eel in your hand,
and you stand on the bridge with your aunt
about to jump. She's your breath
blowing over uncles who didn't exist,
the baby born on the living room floor,
women rushing with water and sheets.
They are in your skin with the boy
practicing bugle, warm bread in the mouth
and salt on the tongue. They are in your laugh.
They sit in your rooms, declare they're in love,
and it's your ear pressed to the door,
the moneylender on the other side, the daughter
locked in the closet, brooms, coats, and stacked cans,
the daughter who was not born. They flush
the skin, live behind the eyes, sink in the throat
with the other loves, the other children,
the wind off the ship, the bark of dogs.
They speak in the ache in the shoulder,
with the fear that lurks in the mute, the son
hanging from the shower rod, the man,
the doves, on the roof, the daughter tripping
on the beach, her children playing in the sand.
They are in your voice with the knives,
the cattle in the street, the race out of town.
It's your gun to the boy's head telling him
to choose, and you're calling out the window,
stopping for dandelions on the side of the road,
bitter leaves and pale roots, and you're

the mandolin shaped like a pear, mother-of-pearl,
swinging away from the world, a woman's hips
stepping in song, pulsed in blood, your beating heart.

The Feast of Saint Joseph

If I could go back to March 19, 1953,
I would find my mother in the crowd,
waiting for the procession to begin.
I would not go up to her, I swear,
I would say nothing. I would be wearing
one of those hats with a net that covers my face,
the kind women wear to church so they won't be seen.

She would not see me. She would see right through me
as she'd glance over her shoulder,
her red hair tucked behind her ear, as mine would be,
and then she'd wave in Italian
at her grandfather, window-washer turned cheese man,
and he'd be standing at the corner with his cart
and sorry horse. At least give me that.

If I could go back, I'd cheer with the crowd,
Italians, Roman Catholics, superstitious and bloody,
Italians from the green and ashy fields of Naples,
whole families, my mother's a family of butchers,
plumbers, and thieves, of good cooks
who dried pasta on the bed, of women
who pinned rosemary to the wall for quick delivery,

women who believed a spider spinning down
meant good luck, time to play the lottery.
And my mother, six years old, in a few weeks seven,
would have already learned the habit of sleep, how easy
it is to slide into, how bouquets of flowers
can take one under. Sleep is exile.
And when she was older, she would say how she slept

from headaches she'd had since a child,
how there was no money, then or now,
how she fell down the fourth floor stairs
of her building on 183, the building
she colored with chalk, and she'd say
how no one found her, how she'd told no one
but me, a child standing at her bed.

So if I could go back to 1953,
to March 19, on Saint Joseph's Feast,
Joseph, patron saint of carpenters and builders,
saint of woodworkers and Italians in New York,
homesick, stubborn Italians,
home of exiles, angels, and ex-cons,
if I could go back to 187th St.

between Southern Blvd. and Arthur Ave.,
then I'd give the Bronx cheer with the crowd
as the church ushers would carry the saint
over the street, a street strung with lights
from block to towering block,
and Joseph, his long, sad face would be carved from wood,
and his velvet cape would be dragged on the ground,

and then, finally the whole scene
could be dipped in blood and forgotten.
This is luxury. The Franciscans coarsely march by me,
brothers linking arms, and the sisters,
with bright faces only,
hold images of the Holy Mother,
her single blessedness, up to the crowd.

What is this procession?
Funeral or parade? Who are these people
wailing and crying? And what am I doing here?
Dirty, drunken Catholics, they spit on Italy,
they spit on Naples, they spit on the ground
that gave them nothing. They gave up whole farms,
family vineyards, and their own stone ovens,

and for what? Someone take the saint's head
and lift it over the street. That will silence them.
The crowd's tossing flowers, carnations, some red,
and roses, the pagans, too much rococo.
The Sons of Italy conduct their brass band,
and look, they're waltzing, they're taking women
from the crowd. This is your serenade.

Poor Joseph, how was it to have your wife
conceive that way? To take that child as your son?
You didn't ask to live with your sheep
and dirty goats always trailing behind you.
They're pinning money to your cloak with their prayers.
These broken Italians, these sleepwalkers, homesick angels,
they thought the roads would be paved with gold,

they came to strike it rich, and they've got nothing,
absolutely nothing to lose. Let me take a dollar bill
and give it to the young man on my left, and say,
See that child with the red hair?
Lift her up, help her pin it to his cloak,
and here's a tip for you,
do it, and then let me disappear.

The Journey

for my grandmother

The horses jingling and stomping their hooves,
the men shuffling their boots on stone flags:
she hears her mother rub and blow on her hands,

the pull of her wool skirt when she steps to her horse.
Still small enough to fit inside harvest baskets,
she climbs onto a wagon bed,

curls herself inside the farthest one,
presses her body into its stiff cords,
the ride down the yellow hill.

Her back to the drivers' voices, her face to the sun,
she watches the houses grow smaller,
the bobbing heads of the donkeys,

their big, lashy eyes. Half-asleep,
she hears her mother call out and knows
they're in the valley, knows her mother's legs

are draped over the horse's side,
her mother is about to spring off,
to take the worn bridle and lead the men

under the trees, to bring in walnuts,
la raccolta, to pull them off
with wire claws, press them into

smooth gold oil, and sell it in town.
Her mother pointing down the rows,
the girl walks away, sits under a tree,

thinking of her sisters still lying in bed,
her father's shiny flute on the mantle,
the cold grass, the dark green leaves,

then the chain of her mother's mourning cross
brushing her face, her mother shaking her shoulders,
afraid of this sleep, the branching tree.

———————

Her mother told her stories:
the four hills of Nicosia,
the cathedral San Nicolò,

the monsignor's palace—
where the black robes of two nuns
raised her like a princess,

never letting her cook or wash or sew.
And maybe one day, walking in the garden,
her mother looked down the hill and told her

about Nebrodi, the name she learned
in a book for the wrinkled blue hills,
about the bishop, his wheat fields, the shimmery heat.

Or maybe she told her how she liked to watch
the swallows fly to the small lake near
Santa Catarina Villarosa, the tiny, embroidered town

where she would one day marry a musician,
a man who could play every part, give lessons
and lead concerts in church squares.

And maybe her mother told her how
her husband was shot by the husband
of one of his other loves, leaving her

with six children and the groves she finally
could not tend. Or maybe she only told her about the trees.
Standing in a window of white almonds,

she told her daughter to go to the square,
to wash spinach in the fountain, to carry dough
to the town oven, to walk not run,

to nod to their neighbors as she stepped
into the kitchen to fry a bundle of thistles,
and maybe the taste was already on her tongue.

—————————

She is thinking of the trip from Santa Catarina,
a two-day train winding through fields
now filling with narcissi, now dry and cracked,

now oak woods, pasture, mountain switchbacks
looking like crooked alleys in so many empty towns.
She is running and thinking of the trip from

Caltanisetta to Marianopoli,
sitting with her mother and sisters,
their train running by Villaba and Valledolmo,

by Ália and the Scalfani Bagni,
by the Montemaggiore Belsito,
and she is running with a basket of fruit and nuts

and thinking of the names she checked off the map,
how she sat with Le Madore on her right
and Caccamo on her left, how the train stopped,

the overnight ferry, how she sat on deck
from Palermo to Napoli.
The harbor brims with boats and voices,

children wandering the wharf, and she's looking for
a sign, the U.S. Mail Steamship Company,
her first English letters to match her first English words.

She's looking over the heads of men
with handkerchiefs full of lemons and women
tightening their shawls, and she's looking towards the sky

when she starts running towards a boat named for a child bride,
running up the plank as if she were running
into the full light of the March sun,

her mother calling, *Giovanna, tuo cesto.*
She turns to catch her mother's voice,
pale and flowering on the dock.

Two

To a Heron

Your body of sticks and light and straw,
you are the season that turns, blue
like flat stones and dirty ice,
the leaves from my muddy childhood trees.
I see your arched wings, the curve of your neck,
and I want to go to the weedy bottoms,
where the brackish water widens,
then slows, and the iris breaks through
like wild stars. My shy one, my quiet one,
my skinny-legs bird, what I don't know of returning,
you are the quick fall into black night.
My ghost, my double, my troubling mind,
you trick the air with your patience,
trace the cool sweep, my stark time.

To a Cicada

One of you sounds like one million,
your rackety music is a thousand screen doors
slamming shut in the night. Someone needs
to oil your wings. You shake the day with your music,
you've infected my dreams. All summer your song
goes on and on until I think you're gone for good,
and then fall, late September, October,
tonight, the first full frost, and you get even louder.
You're the final sweep of the symphony,
the tenor gesturing on stage, the boy practicing
guitar late in the garage. Your terrible static
rumbles in my ears, opens up the cold
breezy night and then the winter storms.
Already I'm lonely without you.

To a Spider

Because you're black and fuzzed and small
and because you map this window
with a bird's eye and monarch's wing,
I'll write a poem for you, thimble
of dusty stars, open boxes, and dirty glass.
Silence's cartographer, you compass
the world with the longitude of a meadow
and the latitude of a stream.
I'll never have your patience,
your quiet, or your full swell of night.
Spider of nobody's chances,
of winter flowers and empty lies,
you're the wind in abandoned houses,
the creak in broken stairs, you stitch
the sky as if you could scaffold the light.

To a Crow

I am black, but Comely,
O ye daughters of Jerusalem.
   —*Song of Solomon*

All morning you stand on the chimney
puffed like some boozy boy. Cawing,
sometimes clicking, you boast and swagger
over the slushy alleys and roofs.
Nobody's sweetheart, you turn towards
the river, the gray horizon, a braid
of smoke, and you shine like the forgotten star
on the night no one wants to remember.
Now you flap instead of glide, your heavy wings,
your awkward body with your shivering sound,
and you're no one, the blank space in the air,
some tree at the city's edge, and you sing
in your soft voice, the voice no one hears.

To a Catalpa

Where have you been, my scraggly one?
Here, in the alley, leaning into the windows,
brushing your icy limbs against bricks?
I hear your creaking in the winter wind
waking the sleepers from their beds.
If you'll blossom for me now, my lonely,
I'll make a house from your branches,
study your gnarled limbs striped in gray and almond-brown.
Words come from your flowers, *head with wings*,
a grammar of snow dusting your heart-shaped leaves.
I want to lie down under your branches
and look out at a sky of Japanese blue.
Your petals fall down in a white perfume
of what we cannot say.

To a Mockingbird

So it's you, sitting on the aerial,
singing an aubade of car alarms and buses,
dogs in the alley, a scratchy record caught in a groove,
singing your love to a foggy city that says "do not disturb."
From your Sunday perch you sing a thin sliver
of river, trains whose winter whistle you echo
along with plane engines, New Year's pots and pans,
the minaret, bells calling the faithful to prayer.
My Russian bird who winds up with a key,
you sing in perfect pitch the songs of cats and sparrows,
of garbage cans and roof-top puddles.
You're an alarm clock without the snooze,
a truck hitting the brakes, a player piano left in the rain,
please, please go back to sleep.

To a Group of Starlings

All day you've chased the nuthatch, the titmouse,
the purple finches in the trees, and now
you strut down the street like overgrown boys,
raccoon coats hiding your matchstick legs,
the sidewalk your grand runway, and you're
boys on newspaper boxes, little drummers
playing buckets and pails, shoe-shine men calling,
hustlers, shiny watches, the old shell game.
Bird of midnight sheen, of oil and ink,
of trashcans in the alley, you're
my hard-times bird, my hand's shadow.
You swarm over the roofs like thought
before it falls, you shoot from the furnace
with the coming rain, dirty stars, faraway flames.

To a Pelican

What are you doing here, my wanderer?
Shouldn't you be flying the dark length
of the Mississippi, the flat fields of worn brooms
and white lights that mark the way to the Gulf?
What storm tossed you in its winds, brought you
to an island ready to fall into marsh and then into the sea?
You swim by the swans like a shy boy at school.
Do you think you're one of them, too?
If you puff your feathers, if you hold
your head straight, then curve your neck,
a birch bending into its leaves, if you put
your beak to your chest and open your eyes
with your sweet love, maybe they'll take you as you are,
lonely moon on the water, light of my distant star.

To a Fly Trapped in a Beach Road Motel

As big as the ball of my thumb,
a knot of shiny thread, you pilot your body
like a rickety plane over this tiny seaside town
with its shacks and souvenirs. I hear your humming,
more like buzzing, and I'm battling the air
for what seems like hours, your weird music
a band of kazoos never getting it right,
the church-goer singing loudest and always off key.
Where do you want to go, my little one,
into the marsh that must be terrible in summer,
the light house beam trembling with the island wind?
I open the door and direct you
like some silly mother and what she knows
of a lullaby into the dark singing, the frozen air.

To a Seagull

Who are you trying to impress, wheeling
through the cold, a starfish dangling from your beak?
No one hears your wailing, your laughing,
no one hears your jokes or your cries.
When you sing your song—the man hanging his nets,
the boys walking their dogs, the low lights
from winter's shacks—even the trees,
the rowboats in the inlet turn away.
My paper kite, my seaside clown,
when you scan the water for the mussel,
the clam, examine a pile of broken shells,
your wings ripple with the shallows. You're
the calm under the dock. You swing into the sky,
sweep down again, late air, my salty light.

To a Black Bird on the Water

So this is how it goes, you on the water,
me on the beach, and we'll make our way
up-island with the plovers heading north?
Sometimes a little in front, sometimes
a little behind, you're a paddleboat
without its wheel, a boot tossed by the waves.
When you dive for the fish, the eel,
I wait with the trees and white dunes.
Cloud's shadow, desert caravan's mirage,
you're a shooting-gallery bird moving
down the line, a lost toy, an empty bottle,
and your voice is the lighthouse's swirl.
Love's secrets, my wooden star,
you sit on the early water like a dark jewel.

To a Snail

My stubborn one, my lovely,
how you inch by the shoes of children,
slide between horses, how you stop
for the slippered feet of women bending
in the garden. Wet and glisteny,
you stretch over the path like bedstraw turning
towards the sun. Where are you going
like a broken top, my curl of the tongue?
If you hide in the shaggy weeds or sleep
in the currants' shade, you can climb
a stem into the tangled air that sits on the leaves
and come down like morning's red weight.
My coat of gray, my quiet star,
you empty the sky of my thin white fields.

To a Cormorant

So you've decided to guard the harbor,
dry your wings and pace the rocks,
watch boats leave and enter the narrows,
two long lines with sails down and motors on?
No one wants you here with your muddy feet.
You dirty the booms. See how they've hung
plastic owls, banging metal rods,
wires strung down and pointing up?
Not the fishermen with their lobsterpots,
the Sunday sailors, or the boys tipping the *Anna Maria*
with the weight of their bamboo rods.
Angel nobody asked for, oil can with wings,
you watch over the water like the devoted,
your quiet love, dark star.

To a Butterfly

The front of your wings piney water,
the back a cold afternoon before the rain,
orange and black and gray, they trace
the stars, line the night with charcoal and string.
My summer's wandering, you navigate
the wind, sail the space between us,
the path's edge, the heavy sky, and now
the yellowing field is too many kisses.
I know nothing of sunsets, of tiny erasures,
of the dust and light that hang in the air.
You're the sap that will crack like memory.
You sleep on a weed, and when I touch you
with a leaf, you open your wings
like a river rising, shut them quick again.

Three

Night Sky

Just when you're drifting in the watery sky,
between the steeple and long ridge, above
the outcrops of rock and the winding roads
that rise and fall like winter's dreams,
maybe when the stars come out one by one,
pin-pricks of light, you'll find yourself
in a story, the way a child takes
a sheet of paper and covers it with
pink and orange swirls and then blackens
the page like a November storm.
With a pin she scratches off the color,
triangles and squares, and the night sky
rises slowly, in quick strokes like speech,
a map of stars—the hill and valley dipping
to the side, the stream running through weeds,
pieces of ice. In the story the world
is green, April, late April because May's too late,
and there's a child sitting on the porch
waiting for dark to fall. It's a story
that has nothing to do with these cold hills,
with its steep slopes and bogs that can swallow
you whole. It's always the same search,
a season's silence, when the earth runs out
of words, when it is just *rock, flint, stone,*
a child falling asleep in the darkening trees,
the creak of wood, the foot on the step.
Finally, all that matters is the sweater
wrapped tight around your arms, the light on the hill
that flickers like a lighthouse or a child
trying to learn the names of the stars.
Then you can hear some dogs, maybe some deer,
and the train pulling its long haul through
what's left of the town. The moment is never
the moment. It's always somewhere else,

that piece of time riding just behind
the hill. You want to get inside the story,
row through the sky with nothing to anchor
but words, as if each letter
were a place to dwell and they'd fit together
in one open sound the way your father
would pick you up and carry your sleeping
body into the open house.

Wedding Kimono

A sour rectangle or damp square,
the box smelled strong and far away,
and inside there was paper, maybe red ink,
and the white tissue my father cut open
when out came cranes sewn in silk and yards
of blue sky thick like a blanket with gold
and silver clouds, long rows of cursive *c*s
curved like a hand or the shape of the world.
My father gave us gifts, tiny books
and paper fans, little kits of towels
and soap from the plane. He was tired,
back from Japan, it was late, my mother,
the kimono on her lap, the papery floor,
and a doll for me, everyone talking.
Outside it was dark, it got dark
later, then night, a few pale stars.
The doll's hair was knotted in large loops
held by combs that looked like bells,
her powdered face, her powdered feet and hands,
her lips a perfect bow, her straight
willowy body wrapped in fabric like a stem.
A garden at night, the wide orange sash
smelled like cloves and burnt leaves.
She's looking far away and listening,
and my father's holding up the kimono,
telling a story about the birds, about the women
selling their robes in the noisy streets,
in a city that is always night, their feathers
splayed across a heavy sky a woman could wear,
put her arms through the red trim, the satin lining,
their wings tipped in black and gray,
their world spinning over swirled water,
their echoing, rattling calls, the spun thread.

49

Winter

The light falling away, the snow blowing off
the pines, the first sting, then cold, then wet:
my mother is pulling the sled and I'm running behind her.

There's the sound of her feet on icy leaves,
the slow dragging of metal runners,
a car on the road below,

and I want to lie on the glossy boards,
drop my hands off the edge, and look up at the trees.
Coming down the hill was my first lesson

in silence, the long space between the oaks,
the moon shining through the clouds,
like foxfire, but softer, like lilac with a few stars.

Say silence rises and falls, has shape like water,
like the small river under the bridge. We watched
the black current, the steam rising, the geese,

only a second, bunched behind a willow,
and then my mother is walking into the woods,
and I'm running towards her leather gloves.

If silence is only the wind widening the air,
opening like fire in the borders of the dark,
then it opens a dark language where rushes

bend in the falling snow and I can stand
with my mother, her breath leaving her body,
the waters of night running under our feet.

Afterlife

They divided them evenly, fifty
for the Narrows, fifty for Brooklyn's
Greenwood Cemetery, Eugene Schieffelin
and his wife released them
from their extravagant wooden cages,
from England and Germany, and finally,
they took. Like too many wishes,
merchants shipped them to Portland and Boston,
imports for Chatham and East Orange, and then
the city of Philadelphia released
one thousand European house sparrows
in the style of a great nineteenth-century
civic show. The idea was to save
the trees from disease, to be reminded of home,
nothing but an empty space, a language
grafted onto the landscape as if
it were a mind. So a gentleman
in Topeka imported five pairs,
and come fall there were twelve, spring
sixty, then three thousand beyond counting.
Nothing went according to plan.
Still the linden moth thrived, the drop worm
and caterpillar gnawed at the leaves
In Central Park a man found four thousand
at one time bathing, and the papers
reported Irish children teaching them tricks.
The house sparrow chose the rail yard grain,
the freight cars, and then,
the story goes, the brakeman shut the door,
locked them inside, and took a train
full of birds across the plains.
Twenty years later *passer domesticus* occupied
one million square miles, at century's turn
an overabundance, the country cursed.

Soon there were spottings in Guadalajara
and Chiapas, then MacKenzie and Manitoba,
while Jesuits introduced them to the selva
and Brazilian mayors gave them as gifts.
European sparrows blew as far
as Tierra del Fuego, stowaways on whaling ships.
Sixty arrived in Australia aboard the *Suffolk*,
nineteen on the *Princess Royal*,
and one hundred and thirty on *Relief*,
the birds marked for a Colonel Champ
at Pentridge Stockade, and soon
the South Australian government paid bonuses
for heads, sixpence a dozen, two shillings
for every twelve eggs to rid themselves
of the pest, while lonely English generals
in Mozambique and Botswana wrote
in their wills that English sparrows should be
released at the hour of their deaths.
The most numerous bird on earth, covering
two-thirds the globe, the entire
temperate zone, chasing out the native
orioles and bluebirds, Whitman's hermit thrush,
choking gutters, spoiling water, their filth
coating shutters and columns,
their clumsy nests holding five to seven eggs,
they are Aristotle's *most wanton bird*,
their coin-sized eggs a pale bluish white,
lilac, dark brown and gray. Bird of endless
brawling, the Anglo-Saxon *spearwe*,
they outsmart the wolf and bear.
The Middle English *lytill foule janglares*
means vulgar, sparrow-mouthed, eating anything
in the littered streets, horses' grain bags,
tenement garbage pails, the rich lamenting
some children knew no other bird,
talk of the seven plagues and who shall
inherit the earth. New York City's poor

foraged in parks, hunted the birds
for roasting, pressed the small bodies
into pastry or corn meal and stuffed
them with wild mushrooms and lime.
If a sparrow taps at the window,
there's a death in the family, if it chirps,
wet weather. Bird of discord and disturbance,
little murderer, you carry thunder
in your feet. *I watch, and am as a sparrow
on the house top.* All day you've been
swirling outside my window, whirling
and dividing into the chimney, shooting out
into the cold, fall air, no shape,
no migratory impulse like the blessed
or forgotten, so fully entering
you are not even here.

Marché aux Oiseaux

The boys stroking the parrot's back, ducks crowded
in the plastic pool, tourists, children putting
their faces to the bars: the man behind the table

looks straight ahead, glasses and scarf around his neck.
He doesn't see the jumbled cages, the narrow aisles,
the reedy nests and ropy houses hung in a row,

doesn't see the trucks, the noisy crates, the people blinking
from the station, their step under the bells, the lights,
onto the wet street. It's as if he's looking and waiting,

looking past the mandarins, their bright beaks,
the plain brown ones bred for their song. Wind in the trees,
he waits for the breeze to lift his hair, winter sun

and warm skin, empty fields, he waits for the water
to relax his feet, run over his legs,
for the season to open like a song, for the woman

pointing before him to take his face in her hands,
turn him towards the sky, her voice a river of birds,
clouds lifting, the underside of a wing.

Dinner with Trimalchio

after Petronius

*Gaius Petronius deserves a further brief notice. He spent his days
sleeping and his nights working and enjoying himself. Industry is the
usual foundation of success, but with him it was idleness.*
—*Tacitus*

Who is this reclining in his litter,
a pipe-playing boy whispering tunes
at his side? I was enjoying the baths,

the pretty boys playing ball, and now
I'm following his offer of a meal,
facing a dog on a chain, his ugly nose

painted on the villa-entrance wall.
My feet, my hands cleaned, my hangnails gone,
a glass of wine, now dormice coated

in honey and poppy, pomegranate
and plum arranged in a fire, and Trimalchio
orders the orchestra to play while two slaves

search through straw for peahens' eggs,
pastry shells we crack with spoons,
yolks of figs and pepper, when cymbals crash

and singing waiters clear our plates,
place a silver skeleton on the table. Trimalchio flings it
into poses, recites his boring poems

before our couch. I'm hungry, tired,
and our applause brings the next course,
the zodiac with chickpeas for Aries,

beef for Taurus, testicles and kidneys
for the Twins, a garland, a fig,
a sow's udder, cheesecake and pastry,

scorpion, sea breams, lobster with a goose
and two mullets, at which we must cry, "Clever!"
Four dancers lift the dish to show Pegasus,

a rabbit with wings, and four statues of Marsyas,
the flayed poet, holding little bottles
of sauce for the fish. What now?

Spartan hounds running round a wild boar,
a freedman's cap between its ears and palm-leaf baskets
hanging from its tusks? Syrian, Thebian dates,

little cake piglets going for its teats?
The carver jabs the boar's side and out flies
thrushes to be caught by fowlers while Trimalchio

drones on about all he owns, how he can walk
Italy's boot and never leave his land,
and who is he trying to impress

with his backed-up bowels? "Don't hold yourself in,"
he snorts, wind in his brain. "God won't object!"
I just wanted to rest, get away from Quartilla,

who covered me with kisses after her greasy boy
got me in the ass. I just want my Giton,
my sweet, to myself, the next town, away

from my friends, the thieves, the plague, the pit,
so we can nestle in bed. I can't be exiled again.
Our host announces pigs for our choosing,

but before we do, he taps the oldest one,
and the meal appears and he starts a debate,
should the cook be whipped for his speed,

when he slices the belly and out rolls sausages,
and he takes a drink. Why am I here?
For Trimalchio's accounts, acrobats, recitations of Homer,

a brazed calf in a helmet on a 200-pound plate?
Prayers for the household gods and a statue
of Trimalchio we must kiss? What's this?

A table dusted with vermilion and saffron,
powdered mica for a sea-urchin dessert
(quinces with thorns), all made by a chef

who makes goose from pork, doves
from ham, and now the boys rubbing our feet
with cream, wrapping our legs in flowers,

and now Trimalchio reading his will, kissing
his slaves, his wife, his slaves, discussing his grave,
the fruits, model ships in full canvas,

the banquet hall he wants for his remains.
He wants another bath. I want to get out
He wants us to praise him as if he were dead,

the trumpeter's dirge, the note so loud
the fire brigade thinks there's a call,
breaks in with water and axes. Here's my chance,

where's the door, let's go, where's my cloak,
I just want the dark drunken night,
the cold air, the sting on my face.

Astor

Sometimes you'll see her stepping off the stairs
into the cold gray light, the noise already
and the garbage, the stairwell wet
with cleanser and piss, passing the men
on St. Mark's, their suitcases roped to someone's
dirty clothes, books swelled with rain,
someone's muddy shoes. April is wind
in dusty shafts, the last chestnuts steamed
in bags, the dark slick in the trees.
Maybe she's sitting on one of the benches
or walking across the square where the sun
hits the buildings streaked with rain.
Someone has bread wrapped in paper, a cup
of coffee, someone walks by a cellar door,
hears a man being beaten down there,
and someone, strung out, skirts the edge of the park.
And if it's true, she's already
lost to herself, always wanting to be
somewhere else, it's a hard music,
an orchestral tapping deep in the blood,
oceanic like a shell to your ear.
What scares you? The constant opening
of a season, a flower that blooms
and blooms, no correspondence, what
you're not able to contain?
Spring means *desire, to jump* as if
she could leap into the season like
the sky's rough clouds or the wind's salty end.
Already the birds shouting in the trees,
starlings or blistery jays, their nests
of rotting ice, as if they could
navigate this space like a difficult love.
Spring means moss on brick, puddles of glass,
weathered steel, the first patch of bluets,

raw sooty skin. You'll never catch
the moment the green dusts the trees, break it
down into all its parts, the glare of soft stone,
the rattle off a winter ash.
It splits like the body haunted by
its other selves like the girl crossing
the street under the first leaves.

Hopkins' Clouds

For Lent. No pudding on Sundays. No tea except if to keep me awake and
then without sugar. Meat only once a day. No verses in Passion Week or on Fridays.
No lunch or meat on Fridays. Not to sit in armchair except can work in no other
way. Ash Wednesday and Good Friday bread and water.
—Notebook, January 23, 1866

were prism-shaped, flat-bottomed, rhomboids.
They were ellipsoid comets.

They were a little ruddled underneath, with fleecy spots.
They moved in rank, not file.

They were great wide-winged or shelved racks of rice.
They were the Monte Rosa range from the Gornergrat.

They were two wagons or loaded trucks,
disheveled and delicately barred.

They were brindled and hatched, curdled and moulded,
painted with a maddery campion-colour

that seemed to stoop and drop. They branched like coral.
They were sopped cake,

a very slim-textured and pale causeway of mare's tail.
They were smooth knots of bamboo, and they were scudlike.

They were slanted flashing "travellers," all in flight,
white napkins thrown up in the sun

but not quite at the same moment, falling one after the other to the ground.
Ribs, girders, wave-tongues,

sometimes jotted with a more bleeding red beneath,
sometimes edgeless soft meridians,

they were great dull ropes coiling overhead and sidelong,
mottles, combs, sprays from spines,

or bright woolpacks, a white shire.
They were transparent, almost straight gauze,

meshy, gray, tretted and mossy.
They were anvil-shaped, flying scarf-ends.

They were bales, blown-flix and zs.
They were frets of fine net in motion, fish-pellets of silver,

spoked, swollen or straight seamed, pitching over.
They were white like the white of egg, and bloated looking.

Dull curds-and-whey with silky lingering,
they were full of eyebrows and spitting rain.

They were heavy cables being paid,
rippling, mealy, chalky, delicately crisped.

They were bulky heads, they were dirty wisps,
dolphin-backed, sail-colored brown and milky blue,

they were the linings of curled leaves one finds in corners of a wood.
They were part-vertical, burly-shouldered, folds and loaves.

They were ringlets of a ram's fleece blowing,
pearly shadows and moist gold dabs.

They were broken into mackerel. They were dappled,
the warp of heaven. They were pied.

Theories of Flight

Yea, the stork in the heaven knoweth her appointed times:
and the turtle and the crane and the swallow observe
the time of their coming.
— The Book of Jeremiah

For some species there was no accounting.
Aristotle knew cranes flew from Scythia to Egypt,
travelers saw them, tracked their flight.
Merchant sailors watched garganeys fly
from Italy to the Nile, spotted eagles
over the water, pintails and wigeons,
but not the thrush or wren, only noted
their salt marsh stagings, and this is where the theories begin:
the large birds ferry the small ones over.
Some birds disappeared, only to reappear
six months later. Nothing could fly off the map,
so redstarts changed into redbreasts, garden warblers
into blackcaps, cuckoos into sparrow-hawks,
while kites slept winters in caves.

Olaus Magnus, Bishop of Uppsala,
said swallows, like swifts and martins,
half-year birds, favored autumn's reedy banks,
sank in mud pulled from thaw
in nets packed with fish. Storks,
said A *Person of Learning and Piety*,
went to the moon, because it was nearest,
fit the Copernican scheme, *gone as soon as found*,
now in the moon, now underground,
and a Cistercian prior decided to ask
a bird the size of his hand, *Oh, Swallow*,
where do you live in winter? Next season
the bird returned, a reply tied to its leg,
In Asia, in the home of Petrus.

What do they know of their returning?
What pulls them into their wings? And what
do they see of their welcome, men with masks
and beaks dragging a boy over the fields,
then one boy a hen, another a cockerel,
one spinning and dancing while the other
throws chaff, a rake at his feet?
The Sami said birds brought back messages
of sickness and death, in Russia
lost children came back as swallows.
In Japan the cuckoo visited the Realm of the Dead,
men exorcised evil spirits by dancing
like cranes, then its song in the Hebrides,
its flight from the Blessed Isles, the first day of spring.

What questions do they answer? What secrets do they bring?
The Tuva said the oriole's first note meant planting,
and the Chipeway said the bluebird
brought summer on its wings, so they named
their months *The Coming of the Birds,*
The Arrival of the Geese, The Month of Birds
Flying Away. Rome north, women caught
forty or fifty swallows ready to fly,
they'd pound them in mortars, add castor oil,
white wine, distill, giving two or three spoonfuls
with sugar for passion of the heart,
passion of the mother, the falling sickness
and sudden fits, the dead palsie, lethargies
and apoplexies, because *it comforteth the brains.*

When did they first fly to return,
when Noah asked the raven, who did not,
the dove's three trips, the swallow bringing back fire?
Some want flight charting memory,
the spreading of continental plates,
memory encoded in genes. Some want flight
carved by ice, water, and a glacier's edge,
the plains covered with wings. Their bodies' rhythms
set to the sun, if caged, they're restless,
face the way they would be moving, bright compass,
they turn their bodies with magnetic fields,
UV and polarized light, the eye a dial, they feel the Coriolis,
fly as high as the air will take them,
following the weather in waves.

What sends them skyward, what electric pulse
runs through their blood? What ignites their bodies,
what startles them from sleep, and what sleeps
in their genes? Some fly only mornings,
from dawn till noon, and some fly all night
like gold-crests and thrushes. Some fly day and night,
in one- and two- and three-day stages, and some,
like swifts and terns, Coleridge's albatross,
never touch down, out of the air at most
three months a year. When they sleep on a reed,
do they jump at the oily water's wind,
the shimmer and cold their synapses fire?
What shadows do they see in their dreaming?
What shadows do they see under their wings?

Necessary Angel

Because the fields were green and wet and cold
and because the ice in my mouth was hibiscus
blooming like a word I did not know,

because the sky came through the windows
and locked all the doors, because the sun
would not set, a dark purple that could swallow

you whole, because the man on the side of the road
pulled his cap over his eyes, I could not see
his eyes, and his words were birds clattering

in the trees. Because the water left gray mud,
mussels, little inlets that went nowhere,
because I could not speak for days, saw him

racing the tide, because the winds shifted
from east to west in the colors of confusion,
and there were no trumpets blaring, no angels

singing, and I wanted to hear his wings
over my shoulder, because I thought
I could see the curve of the world, I thought

my body sang and sang with the dark,
streaked clouds, lights on the water,
sails lit by lanterns clanging in the wind.

White Summer

Rippled, black, and steep,
the hills are a river of sweet
interruption, and the roads rise
and fall like words I don't know, and the trees
are a language I don't know how to imagine.
Now the gray ledge and outcrops striped as if
they were still rock running and flecked
with a silver that does not catch
in the sun, and now the water flowing
into a marshy wood, a screen of rhododendron
that blooms wild in early June.
If there's cattails and rush,
there's loosestrife and rose,
and a white summer's here with the noise
off the pond until there is no sound,
not even a narrow pocket of speech.
August settles on these hills like a dog
lying down to sleep, and the fog sweeps
like the curve of a feather when just as soon
it is gone, a damp haze in the heat.
Always the stone wall sprawling, lacing
the road or digging deep into the woods,
a strict rule bound to break like some barn
or shack left open to warm ruin, a dry spoil.
And always the young trees.
What I want is a field hemmed in stone
on one side, wood on the other, a sudden
place, lush and uninviting, emptied
of patience, an unending motion,
my scattering. There'll be apples,
just blossoms, rocks that will never come out
of the ground, and petals will cover
the grass like snow, a confusion of seasons.
If I'm lucky, there'll be a house,

and inside, on the table, flour and sugar
and salt, a pump at the sink,
and the porch roof will be painted blue
like the surface of a milky pool and above it
an unglittering sky washed of grief.

Muse
Susan Aizenberg

This Country of Mothers
Julianna Baggott

In Search of the Great Dead
Richard Cecil

Names above Houses
Oliver de la Paz

The Star-Spangled Banner
Denise Duhamel

Winter Amnesties
Elton Glaser

Fabulae
Joy Katz

Train to Agra
Vandana Khanna

Crossroads and Unholy Water
Marilene Phipps

Misery Prefigured
J. Allyn Rosser